W9-BHE-186

Environmental Awareness:
SOLID WASTE

AUTHOR
Mary Ellen Snodgrass

EDITED BY
Jody James, Editorial Consultant
Janet Wolanin, Environmental Consultant

DESIGNED AND ILLUSTRATED BY
Vista III Design, Inc.

BANCROFT-SAGE PUBLISHING, INC.
601 Elkcam Circle, Suite C-7, P.O. Box 355,
Marco, Florida 33969-0355

Library of Congress Cataloging-in-Publication Data

Snodgrass, Mary Ellen.
 Environmental awareness—solid waste / by Mary Ellen Snodgrass;
edited by Jody James, Editorial Consultant; Janet Wolanin,
Environmental Science Consultant; illustrated by Vista III Design.
 p. cm.—(Environmental awareness)
 Includes index.
 Summary: Focuses on the ever-growing problem of managing the
many types of solid waste and the hazards they pose to people and the
environment. Readers learn how they can help in waste reduction
efforts.
 ISBN 0-944280-28-5
 1. Refuse and refuse disposal—Juvenile literature. 2. Waste
minimization—Juvenile literature. 3. Recycling (Waste, etc.)—Juvenile
literature. [1. Refuse and refuse disposal. 2. Waste minimization. 3.
Recycling (Waste)] I. James, Jody, Wolanin, Janet. II. Vista III Design. III.
Title. IV. Title: Solid waste. V. Series: Snodgrass, Mary Ellen.
Environmental awareness.
TD792.S65   1991
363.72'85—dc20

**International Standard
Book Number:**
Library Binding 0-944280-28-5

**Library of Congress
Catalog Card Number:**
90-20950
CIP
AC

PHOTO CREDITS
COVER: Vista III Design; John DeMarco p. 32; J.E. Kirk p. 19, 20, 21, 31; K.G.
Melde p. 39; Silver Image, Walter Coker p. 43, Richard Hobbs p. 17, Steve Nesius
p. 4, 22, Steve Morton p. 9; Unicorn Photography, Rich Baker p.13, Wayne Floyd
p. 28, Jean Higgins p. 44, Martha McBride p. 34, Jim Shippee p. 26, Aneal Vohra
p. 15; USAF p. 37; Vista III Design, Ginger Gilderhus p. 16, 18, 25, 29, 30, 44, 45,
Grant Gilderhus p. 10, Jackie Larson p. 33.

TABLE OF CONTENTS

If solid waste keeps growing so rapidly, even the biggest landfill is not going to be able to handle it all.

CHAPTER ONE

COPING WITH WASTE

Each day, every person on earth causes waste. Some of the waste comes from food scraps. Even more comes from wrappers, newspapers, junk mail, cardboard boxes, and other paper goods. In addition, people wear out their clothes and shoes. Children break their toys and bicycles. Cars and appliances stop working. These, too, end up in the scrap heap. When these odds and ends are piled up, **solid waste** quickly becomes a problem.

Most city planners have special places to collect these piles of solid waste. Still, even the biggest landfill cannot hold all the rusting auto frames, worn-out sofas, typewriters, and discarded Christmas trees. How are people going to manage solid waste if it keeps growing so rapidly? Here is what the Sanders family learned about the size of the garbage problem.

Recycle usable household goods.

5

CLEANING THE ATTIC

Curt Sanders and his two buddies coasted up the sidewalk. Their tires squealed to a stop. The boys laid their bikes on the lawn next to the curb and hurried to the side door of the Sanders house.

"Mom," Curt yelled. "Are you home yet?"

"Here I am," Mrs. Sanders called from the top of the attic stairs. "I'm glad you brought Jojo and Andy. Can you boys give me a hand? I have a lot to carry downstairs."

"Sure, Mrs. Sanders. For a lady who makes the best pecan brownies in town, I'll do anything," Andy replied. He smiled sweetly and pulled Jojo along by the front of his T-shirt. "Here are three of the most willing helpers on Wilson Avenue."

Jojo adjusted his radio earphones as he followed Andy and Curt to the dusty attic.

"Whew, Mom," Curt said. "What are you doing with all these boxes of junk?"

"I'm going to take them to the city landfill. Will you boys each carry an armload to the van?" Mrs. Sanders asked.

Mrs. Sanders stopped long enough to brush a cobweb off her forehead. She stacked up several straw hats on an old chair cushion. Then she tossed the pile to Curt. At her feet were four cardboard boxes tied with string. Off to the side stood a broken chest of drawers, some stuffed animals, and a window fan.

"Come on, fellows," Curt ordered as he started down the steps with the straw hats and chair cushion. "If we want any food, we've got to work for it."

For ten minutes, the only sound to be heard at the Sanders house was the clump of feet up and down the attic steps. Then Mrs. Sanders shut the attic door and went downstairs to find her car keys in her purse.

"Who wants to go along to the landfill and help finish the job? All helpers get an extra brownie and milk." She jingled the keys in the air and smiled at Jojo.

"Count me in," Jojo yelled over the sound of rock music from his earphones. Before Mrs. Sanders unlocked her side of the van, the three boys were waiting to climb in the back.

Everyday people create heaps of throw away items,
all destined for our nations landfills.

AT THE LANDFILL

The drive to the city's sanitary landfill was long and dusty. The van bounced over a narrow dirt road past the water treatment plant. At the gate to the landfill, a guard stopped the car.

"Name," he demanded, holding out his clipboard.

"Judy Sanders," Mrs. Sanders answered.

"Address?" the guard asked.

"408 Wilson Avenue," was the reply from Mrs. Sanders.

"What kind of trash are you dumping?" questioned the guard.

"Household items from our attic," she answered.

"Okay. Take the right turn through that fence and throw your load out at marker #11."

"Gee, Mom," Curt whistled. "Look at all the garbage. Where does it come from?"

"People like us, mostly," Mrs. Sanders replied. "People outgrow things and wear things out. It doesn't take long for one family to make a large pile of trash."

While the boys tossed the load of junk beyond marker #11, Mrs. Sanders looked around.

"It seems a shame that this landfill will have to be closed soon. Next time we'll have to drive to the other side of Farnham county."

"Why?" Andy asked. "This place is much closer."

"Look how fast it's filling up," she replied. "Soon there won't be enough room for all the trash. The city is running out of space for its garbage."

"Golly," Jojo muttered. "What is the world going to do if the trash keeps on piling up?"

Many landfills are becoming full and cities are running out of space for their garbage.

Solid waste is not just a problem in cities but also in the rural areas.
This rusting piece of machinery has been abandoned.

CHAPTER TWO

SOLID WASTE AND YOU

That's a good question, Jojo. Why do people make so much trash? Where will large cities put it? How will cities find vacant land for more and larger landfills? How will they pay for the land? What other methods are there for disposing of solid waste? What happens to dangerous waste? These and other questions will help you center your attention on the problem of waste disposal.

PEOPLE AND WASTE

The amount of trash made by ordinary people each day is a growing problem. The tons of garbage caused by our throw away society mounts up. Many products are meant to be used only once. These disposables include ballpoint pens, razors, baby diapers, hospital gowns, and aluminum and foam food containers. The problem of solid waste is serious everywhere. Not only do people in large cities worry about solid waste disposal, but people in the country and on farms also study the problem.

When compared to other nations, Americans do not do a good job of managing solid waste. Countries like Germany and Japan try harder to use products that do not cause waste. They also work harder on finding better ways to dispose of trash. Our nation, too, must start doing a better job of managing solid waste.

IMPROPER DISPOSAL

Many things that people buy are eventually thrown away. Sometimes people are too lazy to take their trash to a **sanitary landfill,** where **sanitation engineers** manage the trash safely and cleanly. Instead, these people dump their trash beside a road, in a ditch, or on a hillside. Often they do not even put their trash in bags or boxes. It spills out in a great mess. These people are **litterers.**

Other lazy people drop one piece of trash at a time. These people are litterers, too. They think nothing of leaving drink cans and bottles, food wrappers, and cigarette butts on the ground. Their garbage spreads over a wide area, especially along roadsides. It leaks decaying food onto the ground. When the wind blows, bits of litter fall into ditches and waterways. The result is ugliness and unhealthy conditions.

The mess that litterers leave behind causes many new problems. Hikers and bicyclists must move carefully around the rusted cans and broken bottles. Small children cannot play in areas where trash endangers them. Piles of trash attract rats, flies, and roaches. The piles breed germs that cause typhus, typhoid, and other diseases. Bags of garbage often spill open, causing an unpleasant smell. Woodlands and meadows no longer look pretty. No one likes the looks or odor of illegal trash dumps.

Hikers and bicyclists must be careful around rusted cans and broken bottles.

People who pollute our land are called litterers. These people dump their trash on our hillsides, roadsides and waterways.

13

Wastes dumped into rivers, on beaches, or down city street drains are also dangerous. Pieces of metal and glass can cut people who swim or wade in the water or walk on the beaches. Rough edges on tin cans and bottles may harm animals. Some animals eat foam from cups and containers. This material can clog their bodies and kill them. Plastic rings from beverage cans may strangle birds. Large amounts of garbage can clog drain lines. As water backs up, it can carry garbage onto people's yards.

Some people try to solve the problem by burning their trash. Burning trash is against the law now in most cities. Smoke from these fires causes air pollution. It makes people cough, and their eyes water and turn red. The odor from trash fires is unpleasant. Also, **aerosol** cans in the burning trash may explode from the pressure of the heating gas inside. Obviously, burning is not a good way for people to dispose of trash.

TOXIC WASTE

Some solid waste contains **toxic waste** and can endanger people for miles around. Toxic waste includes paint, household cleaners, motor oil, and **pesticides.** Rainwater can spread these dangerous wastes into creeks, wells, and farm land. When the wastewater soaks into the earth, it spoils the **ground water.** Because many people depend on ground water for drinking and bathing, the problem of toxic waste is serious.

Toxic waste does other damage. It often causes **fish kills,** as well as injury or death to other animals, birds, and plants. Toxic waste can affect dairy foods, meat, and the fruits and vegetables that we eat. If toxic waste catches fire from lightning or the match of a careless smoker, deadly fumes can fill the air. The smoke from this type of fire is harmful to the eyes, skin, and lungs.

Birds often eat discarded foam cups and containers which can clog their bodies and kill them.

COLLECTING WASTE

In most places, governments decide on the best way to manage solid waste. One of the hardest problems of handling solid waste is collecting it and placing it where it will do the least harm. In many cities, local laws control how all garbage and trash must be packaged and collected.

Some cities give each household large metal or plastic trash cans on wheels. These containers usually have tight-fitting lids that will not blow away in a strong wind or be pushed off by dogs. Other cities provide heavy plastic bags with twist ties or tape to seal them. In still other cities, the residents must purchase their own trash bags and cans. Some of these trash bags are **biodegradable.** That means that they will decay much quicker than ordinary plastic.

Some cities require large metal or plastic trash cans on wheels.

Heavy plastic bags with twist ties are provided by cities for unusable garbage. Other containers are used for recyclable materials.

Special trucks are used for garbage pickup that smash the garbage into the smallest space possible.

Most cities have garbage collectors who pick up cans or bags of garbage from the curb. Because these garbage handlers wear padded clothing and gloves, they can manage sharp objects such as broken glass and rusty metals without getting hurt. These collectors drive special trucks that mash the garbage into the smallest space possible. Some of the truckloads of garbage can weigh up to five tons.

Around factories and businesses, special bins stand beside areas where a large amount of trash is thrown away. The containers are tall so that animals cannot easily climb into them and children cannot play in them. The containers have heavy lids that will not blow open.

Special bins are placed next to businesses and factories where a large amount of trash is thrown away.

When a bin is full, a special truck drives forward and pushes long metal arms into slots along each side of the bin. The bin is then lifted and dumped into the truck.

When a bin is full, a special truck drives forward and pushes long metal arms into slots along each side of the container. These arms swing the bin over the back of the truck. After the trash falls into the garbage truck the arms set the container back in place. The lid automatically snaps shut. The container is now empty and ready for more garbage to be placed into it.

Once the garbage collectors have filled a truck with garbage, they haul it to landfills or **sorting centers.** In some cities, workers at sorting centers divide garbage into non-usable and usable items. Non-usable items are sent on to landfills where they are safely buried. Usable items go into separate bins for **recycling.**

In cities with recycling programs, people must separate their usable items from non-usable items before garbage collectors pick it up.

Once garbage collectors have filled a truck with garbage, they haul it to landfills or sorting centers.

21

At this recycling center the worker is sorting aluminum for reprocessing.

CHAPTER THREE

MANAGING SOLID WASTE

One hope for decreasing the amount of solid waste is through recycling usable items. If people try harder to separate bits of trash, such as newspapers, aluminum, plastics, and cardboard, these items can once again be made useful. Many cities have special bins where citizens can sort trash. Others provide **curbside recycling** containers for each household. By collecting all of the trash of one type, such as green, clear, or brown glass, recycling companies can grind up the trash and make it into new products.

RECYCLING CENTERS

Recycling centers are places where cities can turn solid waste into usable materials. For example, some cities collect old tires, glass, and certain kinds of plastics. Then they crush these materials and mix them into a surface for roads. This method helps cities find new uses for items that were once a disposal problem. If tires are left in landfills, they become breeding grounds for mosquitoes. Also, the thick, oily black smoke from burning tires causes air pollution. By mixing the ground-up rubber tires into a usable topping for roads, the cities dispose of the tires safely. In addition, cities save themselves the cost of more expensive paving materials.

Another good material for recycling is paper. By dissolving ground-up newspaper in water and mixing it with bleach, a recycling plant can flatten, squeeze, and reshape the mixture into useful types of paper. The new paper then reappears as magazines, stationery, paper towels, insulation, animal bedding, paper bags, and cardboard egg cartons.

Metals, too, can be melted down and reused. Recyclers can grind some types of copper and aluminum into tiny bits. These bits are heated and shaped into new products, such as copper pipes for water or air conditioning systems. Also, aluminum can be recycled for cans, toys, and automobile parts. By putting these metals to new uses, the city reduces the amount of solid waste and saves on landfill space.

COMPOSTING

Nature itself makes a large amount of solid waste. Each year homeowners rake leaves, mow grass, and trim tree limbs and branches. Like plastics, paper, and metal, these natural products can be recycled and used to do a great amount of good.

Garden and yard wastes can be ground up, put into a pile and dampened with water. After small amounts of **lime** and soil are added, the mixture will soon begin to decay. These natural wastes will then turn into a loose, dark material called **compost.**

When compost is mixed with fertilizer and heated to kill germs, it becomes valuable. Some cities spread the mixture along roadways or in parks to stop the growth of weeds and enrich the soil. In other places, compost is used to slow **runoff** and prevent **soil erosion.** City workers can use compost in greenhouses to plant seeds. The flowers and shrubs that they grow can be transplanted in new flower beds along city streets. In this way, compost helps make cities beautiful.

Some cities sell their compost to farmers and gardeners, too. The compost helps strengthen weak, sandy soil. In areas where clay makes the soil thick, gummy, and hard to dig, the addition of compost makes the clay lighter. The compost also helps the clay dry out after heavy rains. Earthworms soon make their home in the compost and turn it into healthy and productive soil.

This soil erosion caused by runoff could have been prevented by the use of compost.

This new landfill has recently been opened. Space for new landfills is becoming more difficult to obtain everyday.

LANDFILLS

A large amount of solid waste is not reusable. Some trash, such as plastic wrapping, and aluminum foil, is not biodegradable. It will not decay. Other trash, such as fruit juice cartons, contain more than one kind of material. When trash is made up of a blend of plastic, metal, and paper, the recycler cannot separate it into usable pieces. These types of solid waste must be buried in a landfill.

Landfills are huge holes dug in the earth. The largest landfill in the world is at Fresh Kills, Staten Island, New York. This landfill covers more than 3,000 acres. It is larger than 2,000 football fields. The Fresh Kills landfill handles most of the trash from New York City. This amounts to around 20,000 tons of garbage a day.

KEEPING LANDFILLS SAFE

Even at landfills, solid waste must be managed properly to remain safe. Workers line sanitary landfills with heavy clay or plastic liners. These liners protect ground water or area wells from dangerous liquids. Workers at landfills drive heavy trucks and earth movers.

These machines cover wastes that will not decay, such as car batteries, which contain acid and metals.

As garbage trucks back into a landfill and dump their loads, earth movers push the trash into tight bundles. Scraper blades shove layers of soil on top of the garbage. This covering is necessary to stop the spread of disease, insects, and rats. Also, covering the wastes prevents odors from spreading and helps keep fires from starting.

One problem with landfills is **methane gas,** an odorless gas that collects when living plants and animals die and start to decay. This gas is produced in landfills and can be dangerous. It can explode and cause rapid fires which endanger landfill workers or neighboring forests and towns.

If put to good use, however, methane gas can be valuable. Some sanitary engineers place pipes under the landfill. The gas rises through these pipes into collectors. Because methane gas is a cheap source of energy, it can be used to light, cool, and heat homes and run factories.

RECYCLING LANDFILLS

Many years ago, city trash dumps were ugly heaps of odd-shaped garbage. The trash grew rusty and weeds sprang up around it. Sometimes vines covered the whole pile. Today, however, with proper management, landfills can look like neat landscapes. In time, when landfills become full, they are carefully packed down so they will not cave in. A final thick layer of soil hides all trace of garbage.

Plants and trees are planted so that the landfills can be used for other purposes. Like recycled trash, the land itself is recycled. Because the trash has been properly disposed of and methane gas has been removed, these landfills are clean and safe. A smoothly-covered landfill might make a good place for a playground or park.

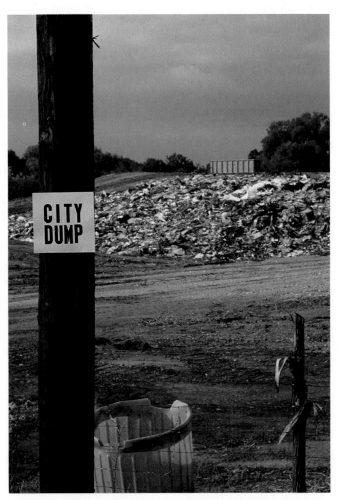

Years ago city dumps were heaps of ugly garbage which polluted the land around it.

This park was once a city landfill. Grass and trees have been planted to make the land usable again.

Because of lack of convenient land available, large cities are having difficulty finding new landfill sites. People don't want landfills next to their homes because of the possibility of toxic wastes, diseases and decreased land values.

Even though properly engineered landfills are safe, neighbors of future landfills are not happy about having garbage dumped near their homes or businesses. People worry about toxic wastes, disease, and decreased land values. They worry that the ground may shift or that their children may fall in a hole in the landfill. Because of these worries, in large cities like Boston, Philadelphia, and Chicago, the search for new landfill areas is becoming more difficult.

Many times new landfills must be located too far away to be useful to people. When trucks have to travel great distances to landfills, they add to heavy traffic. There is then a danger of accidents or spills along the way. Sanitary landfills are expensive to operate. As land becomes more expensive and less available to an area, city planners often look for other ways to deal with solid waste.

Sanitary landfills are often too far away from the city to be useful for most people. When trucks have to travel great distances to landfills, they add to heavy traffic, creating a danger of accidents or spills along the way.

This incinerator, in Minneapolis, Minnesota, burns waste, which produces steam to make electricity.

INCINERATORS

To help solve the problem of solid waste, some cities build large concrete **incinerators** in which to burn wastes. These incinerators use coal, oil, or other fuels to burn trash and garbage. Large trucks or train cars carry the waste to the incinerators.

Within the thick concrete walls of the incinerators, waste handlers place solid waste in a very hot fire. The waste burns quickly to ash. Smoke rises up very tall chimneys, where special **stack scrubbers** remove heavy particles to keep the burning trash from harming nearby people and land.

Acid rain harms plants and animals.

NO EASY ANSWERS

At first, incinerators seemed like the best answer to garbage problems everywhere. Even though they do not burn the solid waste completely, they reduce it to about 10% of its original size. It is much easier to find landfill space for that remaining 10% than for the whole pile of garbage.

Unfortunately, the incinerators also cause some new problems. The chopping and grinding of trash produces too much dust. Some of this dust is made of fine particles of glass and metal. Also, some combinations of garbage create gases that explode when they are burned. Other gases and dust mix with rain water to form **acid rain,** which harms plants and animals. Action committees have begun forming to stop the building of more incinerators.

One point in favor of incinerators is that they produce heat and energy. Some incinerators have water forced through pipes in their walls. The water changes to steam as the temperature rises. This steam is then piped into cities to make electricity or heat buildings.

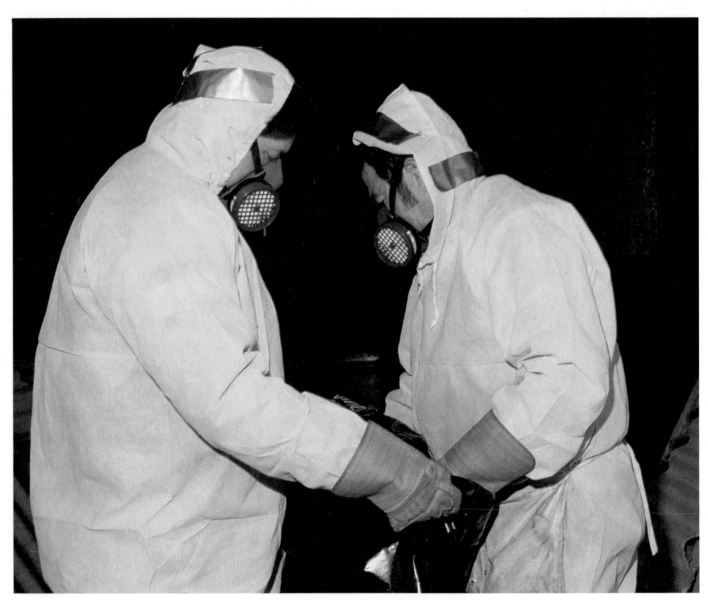

Toxic waste must be handled very carefully by workers in protective suits.

CHAPTER FOUR

INDUSTRIAL, FARM AND MILITARY WASTE

Even though individuals and families make much of the world's waste, factories, institutions, and farms also produce waste. Often the disposal of this garbage requires special care. Another difficulty with factory and farm waste is the cost of collecting and disposing of it. Sometimes the government has to help business people and farmers think of ways to dispose of their solid waste.

BUSINESS WASTE

Large institutions, restaurants, and factories, such as colleges and hospitals, create huge amounts of trash.

Waste from these businesses may be too great a burden for local city planners to manage. Sometimes institutions, restaurants, and factories may have to create their own garbage systems. Often they are forced to ship their waste long distances by truck, barge, or train to a landfill or incinerator that is large enough to manage it.

Some of this waste, such as **heavy metals,** bandages, and human tissue, requires special planning and care. Often, this trash is very dangerous.

Toxic waste and hospital waste must then be burned into ash so that they are less dangerous to the **environment.** For wastes that are deadly, such as some chemicals and heavy metals, waste handlers must use steel drums that will not rust or leak. They bury these drums in a metal-lined hillside. Waste engineers check these drums from time to time. They make sure that none of the dangerous waste inside can escape and hurt people living nearby. Sometimes leaks can occur. If they do they are expensive and difficult to clean up. Still, the collected wastes do not go away. They may remain buried for many years.

Some businesses and institutions recycle garbage. Restaurants, military bases, and schools, for instance, use large amounts of cooking fats and oils. The fats and oils can be cleaned and reused in other forms, such as animal feed.

Other types of factories recycle **by-products.** Furniture factories often mix sawdust with glue and shape it into pressed wood, fireplace logs, or wood paneling. Fabric mills sell their wastes to gas stations. Workers use the cloth for rags to wipe tools clean of grease and oil. In these ways, businesses turn waste into reusable products.

FARM BY-PRODUCTS

Many of the products that come from farms make their own trash or by-products. For example, beef, pork, and chicken processing factories have to dispose of hides, skin, bones, feathers, and parts that humans do not eat. Factories that process eggs, vegetables, and fruit must discard shells, pulp, seeds, and skins. Dairies and canneries create liquids that cause a sour smell and breed germs. These by-products require careful disposal.

Fortunately, farmers and food processors can recycle almost all of their by-products. A large part of the by-products goes back to the farms. Animal parts, spoiled milk, fruit pits, and vegetable skins can be made into natural fertilizer and pet food. Other wastes, such as the pulp from oranges, lemons, and grapefruits, are made into soaps, perfume, and lotions for people or into feed for dairy animals and birds. Some farm by-products are used in glue and cosmetics. Because farmers make good use of their by-products, they reduce the problem of farm waste.

MILITARY WASTES

Another kind of solid waste is the garbage that comes from military bases. These institutions, like farms and hospitals, make their own special type of waste. When airplanes and ships burn fuel, they create dangerous by-products. These wastes, particularly wastes from rocket fuel, are highly explosive and can be deadly to touch or breathe.

Wastes from rocket fuel are highly explosive and can be deadly to touch or breathe.

At one time, some military wastes were dropped into the ocean. Then some of the waste began to wash up on beaches. Environmental groups forced the government to think about the harm these wastes were doing to the earth. Recently, the government has been more careful to keep the ocean clean. Now most military waste is enclosed in drums and buried in the earth.

RADIOACTIVE WASTE

Probably the most dangerous type of waste in the world comes from **radioactive** material. This waste is produced by **nuclear power plants** and submarines that run on nuclear energy. Radioactive waste remains dangerous for thousands of years. It can cause a deadly form of poisoning. People put this waste in containers lined with lead and bury it deep in the earth.

CONTROLLING SOLID WASTE

Solid waste is a problem that won't go away. The **Environmental Protection Agency (EPA)** is the government office that helps control the problem. To protect people and the land, the EPA checks ash from incinerators. The EPA also watches places where toxic or radioactive wastes are stored. The EPA tries to stop heavy metals or harmful chemicals from polluting air and water.

Another important job of the EPA is to protect garbage workers from coming in contact with dangerous wastes. The EPA requires workers to wear ear plugs and goggles for protection. Also, it checks work suits to be sure they are thick enough to keep out harmful liquids and sharp pieces of garbage. When workers enter thick clouds of dust or gas, the EPA requires them to wear masks. Sometimes these workers must wear single-piece suits to cover their entire bodies. In these ways, workers can safely manage solid waste.

Radioactive waste produced by nuclear power plants is probably the most dangerous type of waste in the world.

Recycle usable materials such as newspaper and help save our environment.

CHAPTER FIVE

YOUR PART

Curt Sanders and his friends were concerned about the growing problem of solid waste disposal in their area. They contacted the EPA and local environmental groups to find out what they could do to help.

Ms. Gillian, the chairperson of one local group, told the boys that people cannot stop making waste. As long as there are homes, farms, and businesses, there will be garbage. However, each person can create less waste and be more careful about disposing of it. Also, people can be more aware of the manner in which businesses and institutions dispose of solid waste. Here are the suggestions Ms. Gillian gave Curt and his friends. You and your friends can apply these suggestions, too.

RESTRICT WASTE

1. Buy quality products that will last a long time.
2. Select packages that are less wasteful. Avoid using aluminum foil, foam products, and plastics that are not biodegradable.
3. Reuse paper by writing or drawing on the back.
4. Recycle usable materials, such as glass, newspaper, cardboard, and aluminum foil and cans.
5. Rip discarded cloth into rags for messy jobs. Use rags or washable towels instead of paper towels.
6. Donate used clothing, toys, bedding, and towels to needy people.
7. Avoid metallic wrapping paper and ribbons. Instead, choose light tissue and decorate it with water-based markers.
8. Stop junk mail. Call toll-free company numbers and ask that your name be taken off mailing lists. Write across company postcards: "Take my name off your mailing list."

HALT LITTER

1. Remove trash from roadways, recreation areas, and stream banks.
2. Make certain that paper goods and other trash do not blow away from boats, picnic tables, and cars.
3. Establish containers for recycling aluminum cans, glass, plastic, paper, and cardboard. Take these items to a recycling center so that they can be reused rather than thrown away.

HELP KEEP THE ENVIRONMENT CLEAN AND SAFE

1. Place trash in sturdy bags or in cans that have tight-fitting lids. Tie bag tops securely.
2. Dispose of trash at curbside on collection days. Keep your dog away from garbage so that it will not tear open trash bags or turn over cans.
3. Volunteer to remove litter or garbage from a roadway or beach.
4. Use a litter bag in your car. Empty it at a roadside trash can.
5. Never release a helium balloon into the sky. It causes litter and can interfere with electric power.
6. Cut open the plastic rings that bind beverage cans to prevent animals from becoming entangled in them.
7. Dispose of paint, used oil, pesticides, aerosol cans, batteries, and other pollutants safely. Dispose of dangerous materials according to local, state, and federal guidelines.
8. Insist on biodegradable products.
9. Read labels to be sure that the products you buy are not harmful to the environment.

These people have volunteered to remove trash from a public beach in Florida. The trash is being separated for recycling.

Trash pollutes many streams and ponds.

ENCOURAGE GOVERNMENT OFFICIALS TO TAKE ACTION

1. Write or call local officials or state or national representatives. Encourage them to vote for laws that promote better handling of waste, especially toxic and radioactive waste. Insist on heavy fines to stop littering and illegal dumping.
2. Support citizen's groups, such as those that clean roadsides, stream banks, or beaches.
3. Observe streams and ponds near your home. Report any unusual changes, such as fish kills, dumping, floating trash, oilslicks, or foul smells.
4. Organize a letter-writing campaign to bring dangerous situations to the attention of officials.

ENCOURAGE INDUSTRY TO RECYCLE

1. Buy recycled products or products packaged in recycled materials.
2. Ask questions. Read articles about solid waste and recycling. By learning more, you can be an effective voice for waste control.
3. Write thank-you notes to companies that recycle.

These items have been made from recycled material.

4

GLOSSARY

acid rain (A sihd RAYN)   moisture that mixes with pollution in the air and falls to the earth as rain or snow

aerosol (AYR uh sahl)   a liquid sprayed from a can containing pressurized gas

biodegradable (by oh dih GRAYD uh buhl)   capable of breaking down into harmless products

by-products (BY prahd uhkts)   waste products made by a factory or farm while it is creating useful goods

compost (KAHM pohst)   decayed plant material that can be used to enrich the soil

curbside recycling (KURB sid ree SY klihng)   the pick-up from homes by special trucks with bins for newspaper, aluminum cans, plastic containers, and different colored glass

environment (ihn VYRN mihnt)   the surroundings and influences in which any living thing lives, grows, or develops

Environmental Protection Agency (EPA)   a government office responsible for guarding our country from pollution

fish kills (FIHSH KIHLZ) the sudden death of great numbers of fish due to a change in the environment

ground water (GROWND waht uhr)   water that collects below the earth's surface and feeds wells and springs

heavy metals (HEHV ee MEHT uhlz)   metals, including zinc, mercury, lead, chromium, and arsenic, which can poison humans and animals

incinerators (ihn SIHN uh ray tuhrz)   furnaces that burn trash

lime (LYM)   a substance that helps plant matter decay

litterers (LIHT uhr uhrz)   people who carelessly drop waste on the ground or in the water instead of in a garbage can

methane gas (MEHTH ayn GAS)   an odorless gas that results from the decay of once-living things

nuclear power plants (NOO klee uhr POW uhr PLANTZ) places where tiny particles are broken down to produce energy that can be used to power homes and factories

pesticides (PEHS tih sydz)   chemicals that kill unwanted insects and other pests

radioactive (ray dee oh AK tihv)   giving off harmful particles or rays

recycling (ree SY klihng)   the reuse of discarded items; for example, old tires can be ground into a topping for roads

recycling center (ree SY klihng SIHN tuhrz)   a place where reusable materials, such as newspaper, glass, and aluminum cans, are collected and sorted for reuse in another form

runoff (RUHN ahf)   soil particles that are carried downhill by rain or melting snow

sanitary landfill (SAN ih tar ee LAND fihl)   an area where garbage is safely buried in lined pits away from water supplies

sanitation engineer (san ih TAY shuhn ihn jih NEER)   a public employee who promotes good health by maintaining clean conditions and preventing disease

soil erosion (SOYL ee ROH zhuhn)   the loss of topsoil after roots and other supports are destroyed

solid waste (SAHL ihd WAYST)   garbage and trash such as old appliances, cardboard boxes, and broken or worn-out household items that people throw away

sorting centers (SORT ihng SIHN tuhrz)   places where recyclable items are removed from trash

stack scrubbers (STAK skruhb erz)   devices that reduce the number of particles escaping in steam

toxic waste (TAHK sihk WAYST)   waste that can poison living things